Incredible Insects

by Lisa M. Herrington

Content Consultant

Dr. Lucy Spelman
Zoological Medicine Specialist

Reading Consultant

Jeanne M. Clidas, Ph.D.
Reading Specialist

Children's Press®
An Imprint of Scholastic Inc.

Library of Congress Cataloging-in-Publication Data
Herrington, Lisa M., author.
Incredible insects/by Lisa M. Herrington.
    pages cm. — (Rookie read about science. Strange animals)
Summary: "Introduces the reader to incredible insects." — Provided by publisher.
Includes index.
ISBN 978-0-531-22602-5 (library binding) — ISBN 978-0-531-22748-0 (pbk.)
    1. Insects—Miscellanea—Juvenile literature. 2. Children's questions and answers.
I. Title.
QL467.2.H47 2016
    595.702—dc23   2015021144

Produced by Spooky Cheetah Press
Design by Keith Plechaty

© 2016 by Scholastic Inc.

Printed in China 62

SCHOLASTIC, CHILDREN'S PRESS, ROOKIE READ-ABOUT®, and associated logos
are trademarks and/or registered trademarks of Scholastic Inc.

1 2 3 4 5 6 7 8 9 10 R 25 24 23 22 21 20 19 18 17 16

Table of Contents

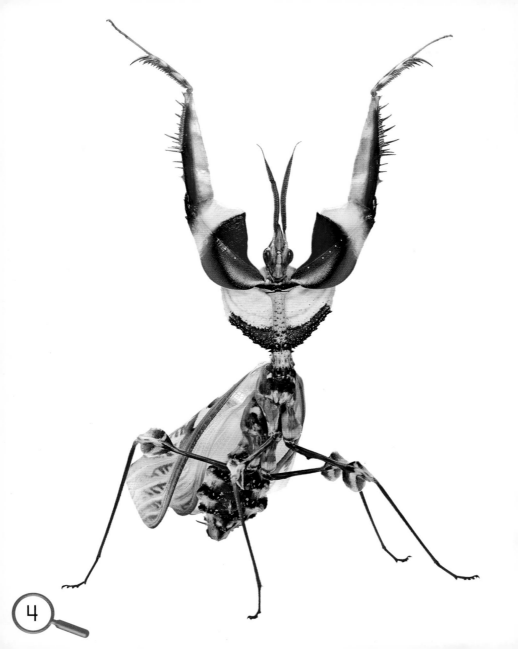

That's Incredible!

Is this an alien? No! It is an insect. This praying mantis stands tall to scare away **predators**.

Strange insects like this *seem* like they are from another planet. But they are really just out of this world!

Insects have three main body parts. They are the head, thorax, and abdomen. Insects also have six legs. They use their antennas to smell and feel. Most insects have wings to fly.

FUN FACT!

Spiders are not insects. They are arachnids (ah-RAK-nidz). Spiders have eight legs and two main body parts.

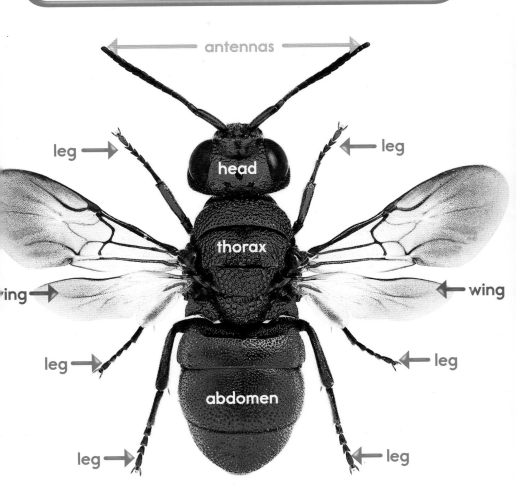

antennas

leg

head

leg

thorax

wing

wing

leg

leg

abdomen

leg

leg

7

Staying Safe

Insects are small. They are often in danger of being eaten. They have many ways to escape danger, though.

This thorny katydid, for example, has sharp spikes.

A katydid is a type of grasshopper.

Watch out! Some insects will really take you by surprise! The bombardier beetle sprays boiling-hot liquid at predators. And get a whiff of this: Stinkbugs let out a bad smell if danger is near.

bombardier beetle

11

slug caterpillar

foaming grasshopper

Many insects show they are unsafe to eat. Bright colors can mean that they are **poisonous**. Some caterpillars are covered in spikes full of poison. Hungry birds know to leave them alone.

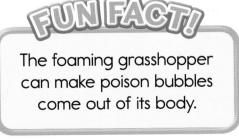

FUN FACT!

The foaming grasshopper can make poison bubbles come out of its body.

Tricky Critters

Many insects use **camouflage** to hide from predators. They blend in with their surroundings. Thorn bugs look like thorns on a twig. Stick insects look like sticks. A green shield bug is hard to see on a leaf.

Stick insects are the world's longest insects. The longest one is about the length of three pencils.

14

thorn bugs

stick insect

green
shield bug

15

Atlas moth

spicebush swallowtail
caterpillar

Some insects copy a more dangerous animal. The tips of an Atlas moth's wings look like snake faces! Some caterpillars can really look like snakes.

Caterpillars are baby insects. They change into adult butterflies and moths.

What's for Dinner?

Insects eat different things. Bees, moths, and butterflies sip nectar from flowers. Many insects eat other insects.

The assassin bug bites its **prey.** It injects poison. Then it slurps up its victim's insides.

assassin bug

Dragonflies are fierce hunters.
They catch mosquitoes while flying.
They can hover in the air like
a helicopter. They sometimes fly
as fast as a car.

Leafcutter ants act like gardeners. The fungus they eat grows on leaves. So they slice through the leaves with their sharp jaws. Then they carry the leaves back to their nest and make a garden.

FUN FACT!

Most ants live in groups called colonies.

A leafcutter ant can carry more than three times its body weight.

24

Strange Finds

Experts think there might be 30 million types of insects that have not yet been discovered. Scientists are always finding new ones, like this planthopper.

There is no doubt about it. Insects are incredible!

Which Is Stranger?

elephant weevil

- The elephant weevil uses its long nose to drill holes into plants. It then feeds on the plants or lays eggs inside.

- Weevils are considered pests. They eat the plants that farmers grow.

You Decide!

treehopper

- Treehoppers come in many shapes. They can look like leaves, thorns—or even helicopters, like this one.

- Scientists are not sure why helicopter treehoppers are shaped this way. They think the shape may scare predators away.

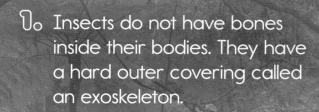

TOP 5 Facts
About Insects

1. Insects do not have bones inside their bodies. They have a hard outer covering called an exoskeleton.

2. Insects are cold-blooded. Their body temperature is the same as the air around them.

3. Insects build amazing homes! Termites make nests that can be taller than three people standing on top of each other.

4. There are more insects than any other animal on Earth. About a million different types have been discovered so far.

5. Nearly two billion people around the world eat insects—from grasshoppers to cockroaches.

Record Holders

Strongest
The Hercules beetle can carry 850 times its own body weight. An elephant can only carry about 1½ times its body weight.

Heaviest
The Goliath beetle can weigh as much as an apple! It can also grow as big as your hand.

Animal
CRACK-UPS

Is this a daddy longneck? No! It is a giraffe weevil. This insect lives in Madagascar, an island c Africa. Males have longer neck than females do. Males use the necks to fight with each other over females. They also use their necks to roll leaves. The females lay their eggs inside.

JOKES

1. **What do wasps like to wear?**

2. **What did the grasshopper say to the praying mantis?**

Answers: 1. Yellow jackets! 2. Bug off!

Glossary

camouflage (KAM-uh-flahzh): when an animal uses color, pattern, or shape to blend in with its surroundings

poisonous (POY-zuhn-us): able to kill or harm if swallowed, breathed in, or even touched

predators (PRED-uh-turs): animals that hunt other animals for food

prey (PRAY): animal that is hunted for food

Index

Facts for Now

Visit this Scholastic Web site for more information on insects:
www.factsfornow.scholastic.com
Enter the keyword **Insects**

About the Author

Lisa M. Herrington loves writing books about animals for kids. She lives in Trumbull, Connecticut, with her husband, Ryan, and daughter, Caroline.